A Miscellany of

MOTHER'S WISDOM

A Miscellany of

MOTHER'S
WISDOM

Nina Grunfeld

HarperCollins*Publishers*

First published in 1994 by HarperCollins Publishers
Copyright © 1991 by Jackson Day Jennings Ltd/Inklink

A catalogue record for this book is available from the British Library.

ISBN 0 00 412931-8

A Miscellany of Mother's Wisdom
Compiled and arranged by Nina Grunfeld
Designed by Simon Jennings
Jacket Design by Simon Jennings
Design Assistant Louise Scovell
Text edited by Peter Leek
Illustrations & engravings enhanced by Robin Harris

Produced, edited, and designed by Inklink,
Greenwich, London, England
Published in the United States by Running Press,
Philadelphia, Pennsylvania
Typeset in Garamond by Inklink
Printed in Hong Kong by South Sea International Press.

A MISCELLANY OF

MOTHER'S WISDOM

TABLE OF

CONTENTS

ARRANGED IN SEVEN CHAPTERS

"How often do we not see children ruined through the virtues, real or supposed, of their parents?"

SAMUEL BUTLER (1612-80)

ONCE MY SECOND CHILD WAS A YEAR OLD, *my natural maternal instincts became stronger and I began to trust them more and more. I found that I could view dispassionately the books to which I had once avidly turned for comfort and advice. As I looked at those books anew, I realized how little the anxieties of parents have changed over the centuries. It also struck me how the advice given to parents has contradicted itself over and over again, until it has gone full circle several times.*

One of the books I came across in my adventures, and have quoted from, was ADVICE TO A MOTHER *by Pye Henry Chavasse. It was written around the turn of the century, when boys were boys and girls were girls. Although his book is filled with advice that has long since been superseded, Chavasse's calm, sensible approach – endorsing fresh air, early nights, manners, and respect for the child as an individual – seemed delightfully reassuring in view of many of the parenting books written today.*

Unfortunately (or perhaps fortunately) child rearing is not a science, and there aren't any "right" answers to many of the problems that parents find trying or baffling. Indeed, very often the right answer is simply to trust your own instincts and do the best you can. Nevertheless, with patience and a sense of humour, most of us survive the challenges of parenthood relatively unscathed – and with a little LOVE, ATTENTION *and* GUIDANCE *our children turn out fine.*

Throughout this book the child is referred to as "he". I chose this pronoun for the sake of simplicity, since the mother is always female.

Nina Grunfeld

NINA GRUNFELD

A CHILD IS
THE BRIGHTEST RAY
IN THE SUNSHINE OF
A PARENT'S HEART

1

PREGNANCY AND BIRTH

F or many women, the news that they are
pregnant represents the realization of their most
cherished wish. *PREGNANCY* is a very special time for
a woman, and  *CHILDBIRTH* the
beginning of a new life – not
just for the child but for
the parents too.

Where did you come from, baby dear?
Out of everywhere into here ...
Where did you get that little tear?
I found it waiting when I got here.

From AT THE BACK OF THE NORTH WIND
by GEORGE MACDONALD (1824-1905)

FIRST YOU HAVE TO GET PREGNANT

Since time immemorial couples longing to have children have resorted to fertility aids. The Australian Aboriginals place beautiful wooden birds and decorated sticks in the room of a couple striving for conception. In England, for those who are desperate, there is always the Cerne Abbas giant, a 180ft-long symbol of virility carved into the side of a hill some 1,500 years ago during the Roman occupation. Legend has it that if a couple make love on his penis a child will be born to them within nine months.

According to modern wisdom, the first step is for the man to avoid very hot baths, alcohol, and wearing tight trousers. The woman should avoid alcohol, too. Both parties should try to relax as much as possible, attempt to revive their first fine, careless rapture, and forget the potentially obsessive reason for now having contraception-free sex.

"Thousands of women are rendered unfit for marriage by what they suffer as the result of tight lacing...The womb, which God has meant to stand nearly upright, is pressed out of position, oftentimes falls either backward or forward, producing such a displacement of the internal sexual organs as to render its victim wholly unfit for the marriage relation, converting an act which at least should not be disagreeable to her, into one of actual discomfort, and oftentimes of positive misery."

From WHAT A YOUNG MAN OUGHT TO KNOW by SYLVANUS STALL, 1904

SAFEGUARDS AND SUPERSTITIONS

In the not so distant past, and in some parts of the world today, pregnant women were believed to be extremely vulnerable to demons, witches and any other form of evil they were likely to encounter. The unborn baby was also at risk as was anyone else in close contact with the mother-to-be.

There were many superstitions about what would befall the baby if the mother did certain things. If she stepped over a grave the baby would die; if she saw a hare the baby would be born with a hare-lip; if she put her hands in dirty water the child would have rough, unattractive hands; and if she touched too many flowers the new baby would have no sense of smell. Even today it is thought to be unlucky to bring a cradle or new pram into the house before the baby has been born.

All these beliefs meant there had to be some good-luck charms to counteract them. As soon as a pregnancy was announced, the mother-to-be would receive countless symbols of luck from nervous friends and relatives. She would have iron nails hammered into her bed, since iron was believed to be a magic metal; and many amulets and stones would be presented to her, the most precious of these being an eagle stone, which was supposed to protect her until the baby was safely delivered.

EAGLE STONE A hollow egg-shaped nodule of clay iron-stone, said to be found in an eagle's nest and to possess magical qualities.

COPING WITH MORNING SICKNESS

If you are suffering from morning sickness:–

Eat a little and often • Eat ice cream or plain baked potatoes • Have a cup of tea or coffee and a biscuit before getting up in the morning • Drink fizzy mineral water • Drink a teaspoonful of bicarbonate of soda in half a glass of water on waking • Try wearing cloth wristbands designed to prevent travel sickness.

"I do think a woman em beraso [pregnant] has a hard time of it, some sickness all the time, heart-burn, head-ache, cramp, etcetera. After all, this thing of marrying is not what it is cracked up to be."
From THE DIARY OF SUSAN MAGOFFIN, 1846

KEEPING FIT

To look after your health:–

Drink plenty of water to keep the bowels regular and the kidneys working • Keep clean, wash regularly • Don't wear tight clothing • Keep up any regular exercise you take for as long as you can • Go for a walk every day • Don't stand if you can sit, don't sit if you can lie • Rest for an hour a day with your feet above your body • Eat regular, good, healthy meals • Do not lift heavy things or stretch your arms above your head • Try to keep cheerful • Visit your doctor (and dentist) for regular check-ups.

STACKING THE ODDS

Although the sex of a child is determined at the moment of conception by the father-to-be, there are still women around the world who try to influence whether the child will be a boy or a girl. It is widely believed that douching with vinegar or lemon juice before intercourse results in a male child, but there is no conclusive scientific evidence to support this.

What are little boys made of, made of?
What are little boys made of?
Frogs and snails
And puppy-dogs' tails,
That's what little boys are made of.

What are little girls made of, made of?
What are little girls made of?
Sugar and spice
And all things nice,
That's what little girls are made of.

NURSERY RHYME

THE TELLTALE HEART

These days there are medical techniques that can reliably tell the sex of the child *in utero*, but before these existed doctors had to use more basic methods. Although not very accurate, counting the baby's heart rate in the uterus is probably the simplest way of determining sex. The normal rate is between 120 and 160 beats per minute. If the foetus' heart averages less than 140 beats per minute, the chances are that the baby is male; if it averages above 140 beats per minute, then the odds are it's female.

PENDULUM POWER

There are also numerous folk traditions about whether or not the baby is a boy or a girl. Dangling an object (preferably the pregnant woman's wedding ring hung on a thread or one of her hairs) over her abdomen is believed to indicate the baby's sex. If it swings in a clockwise direction that means the child is going to be a boy; if anti-clockwise, a girl. Some look at the shape of the expectant mother – at her nose, her fingers, or her belly. A small belly indicates a girl, a large belly a boy, and so on.

Perhaps the most delightful belief is from Sri Lanka, where it is said that if the mother looks particularly pretty she is carrying a girl.

SEXING THE FOETUS

"Put the urine of the woman into a glass bottle, let it stand tightly stoppered for two days, then strain it through a fine cloth, and you will find little animals in it. If they are red, it is a male, but if white, it is a female...The most certain sign...is the motion of the child, for the male moves in the third month, and the female not until the fourth."

From THE MASTERPIECE by "ARISTOTLE, THE FAMOUS PHILOSOPHER"

WAITING FOR BABY

The last weeks of pregnancy can seem the longest, and in the past women who could afford it tended to take to their beds when they thought their time was near. Since there was no way of accurately estimating when the baby would arrive, they often spent as long as three months "lying in", waiting for the birth.

In affluent households a nurse-midwife arrived well before the delivery, months in some cases, in order to be on hand in case the baby was premature. When one royal midwife complained that she was losing other jobs while she waited, the king granted her a handsome sum to cover the loss.

ATTENDANTS AT THE BIRTH

Until quite recently there were only females present at a birth. They were usually friends and neighbours – including the child's female god-parents, who needed to be there as baptism took place as soon as possible after the delivery. Male midwives and doctors were available, but were only sent for if labour was difficult. The husband was banished to another part of the house – unlike today, when it is the norm for the husband, if not the children, to attend the birth.

INDUCING LABOUR

If you simply cannot wait any longer:–

Have a good laugh (watch a funny film on TV) • Go for a very long walk • Go for a bumpy car ride • Pray for a stormy night (more babies are said to be born in storms than at any other time) • Pray for the moon to change or for the new moon to come in (many believe that this is when births are most likely to occur).

SCIENTIFIC PREPARATIONS

"Some female friend of your mamma's (I forget whom) used to say it [giving birth] was no more than a jog of the elbow. The material thing is to have scientific aid in readiness, that if any thing uncommon takes place it may be redressed on the spot…"

THOMAS JEFFERSON, TO HIS DAUGHTER MARY, 1779

THE DAY OF BIRTH

There are many beliefs concerning the day on which the child is born. In some parts of the world it is believed that his whole life and character are determined by the time of his birth. Each day of the week has its own meaning, each month its own birth-stone. There are both Western and Eastern systems for casting horoscopes – and if you are a Buddhist, the sound with which your child's name should begin is determined by the day and time of his birth.

> *Monday's child is fair of face,*
> *Tuesday's child is full of grace,*
> *Wednesday's child is full of woe,*
> *Thursday's child has far to go,*
> *Friday's child is loving and giving,*
> *Saturday's child works hard for its living,*
> *And a child that is born on the Sabbath day*
> *Is fair and wise and good and gay.*
>
> NURSERY RHYME

BIRTHSTONES

January
Garnet – the stone of truth and constancy.
February
Amethyst – for sincerity.
March
Bloodstone – brings courage and wit to the wearer.
April
Diamond – signifies innocence and light.
May
Emerald – for luck in love.
June
Agate – brings good health;
or pearl – for purity.
July
Carnelian – brings peace of mind;
or ruby – for courage.
August
Sardonyx – for a happy marriage.
September
Sapphire – has magical properties.
October
Opal – brings hope for those born in October;
for everyone else, it brings misfortune.
November
Topaz – signifies fidelity.
December
Turquoise – brings wealth.

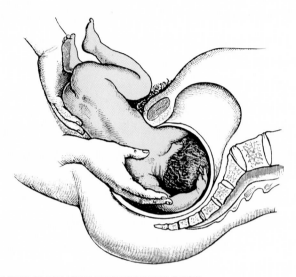

THAT'S NOT THE RIGHT WAY OUT!

In the past, most children born in an unusual manner were thought to have special gifts. "Footlings" (people born feet first), for example, were believed to be able to cure rheumatism, lumbago, backache and all manner of aches and sprains, and they would often be asked to rub their feet against the affected parts of a sufferer's body. Children born by Caesarian section were expected to be exceptionally strong throughout their life, and also to have the ability to see spirits and find buried treasure.

GOOD-LUCK CAULS

A child who is born with his head covered by thin membranes, known as a "caul," will be lucky in life and never drowned, provided the caul is kept. If the caul is sold, the luck will pass to the new owner – so midwives used to sell cauls to sailors as a protection against drowning. David Copperfield is described as having allegedly been born in a complete caul, and as late as 1848 ex-sailors would place advertisements in *The Times* offering the same good-luck cauls for sale that had saved them from a watery grave.

CUTTING THE NAVEL STRING

A seventeenth-century midwives' book, written by a midwife of some thirty years' experience named Jane Sharpe, suggested that the child's umbilical cord should be cut about four finger-breadths from the baby and wiped with a piece of charred linen (to kill germs) before being wrapped in a clean cotton cloth.

Some authorities maintained that the stump of the "navel string" should be left longer for a boy, so both his tongue and his penis would grow long (the males would thus be "well-provided for the encounters of Venus"), whereas a girl's stump should be "tied short".

If the umbilical cord touched the ground, it was said, the child would never hold his water, either sleeping or waking. It was also believed that wearing a piece of navel string next to the skin would protect the wearer from falling sickness and convulsions.

SALT, WINE OR WATER?

The earliest records show babies being cleaned by rubbing salt into their skin – which acted as a mild antiseptic, although it no doubt caused skin irritation. Salt remained a popular cleansing agent in England up to the eighteenth century, when warm water was preferred. In her book on midwifery, Jane Sharpe stated that she washed ruddy-cheeked, healthy babies in wine (which would also have had antiseptic properties), and only used water if the baby seemed white and limp or unlikely to survive. After cleansing them, she would rub the babies "regardless of lust-iness" with acorn oil before swaddling.

TIED TO THE KITCHEN SINK

Besides having sexual associations, the umbilical cord also seems to have had implications for gender. The cord of an Aztec boy, for example, was taken by a warrior and buried on the site of a battle – whereas his sister's cord was buried at home, signifying that she was not free to wander.

KEEPING THE SPIRITS AT BAY

The interval between birth and baptism was considered a dangerous period, during which the child was prey to all sorts of evil spirits. Protective objects – such as a pinch of salt, a clove of garlic, some iron nails or a knife – would be placed in the cradle. In Scotland the mother's petticoat was placed over a boy child, the father's coat over a girl.

BAPTIZE ME FIRST

In 1795 the parish priest of two of the Orkney islands, off the coast of Scotland, complained that:

"Within these last seven years, the minister has twice been interrupted in administering baptism to a female child, before a male child, who was baptized immediately after. When the service was over, he was gravely told he had done very wrong; for, as the female child was the first baptized, she would, on her coming to the years of discretion, most certainly have a strong beard, and the boy would have none."

FROM THE JOURNAL OF AN ORKNEY MINISTER, 1795

PLAYING IT SAFE

As Mark Twain found out, suggesting an appropriate name for a baby can be tricky:

"Mrs. A. once tried to embarrass me in the presence of company by asking me to name her baby, when she was well aware that I didn't know the sex of that Phenomenon. But I told her to call it Frances, and spell it to suit herself."

MARK TWAIN, IN A LETTER, 1862

INTO THE LIGHT

For the first few days of his life the baby was kept in a darkened room, since his eyes were believed to be sensitive to light and exposure to bright light was thought to cause squinting. Most babies today are born under bright hospital lights – but a dark, cozy environment helps the mother relax and is now recommended by some practitioners.

CONTINUED CONFINEMENT

In the fifteenth century mothers were confined to bed for as long as four weeks after the baby was born. For many weeks the threat of the mother dying from childbirth fever was very real, so she was kept warm and sedentary. After a week or so, if she made good progress, she was allowed to sit up. This was often celebrated by a party known as "the lady's upsitting feast". The new mother's first outing would take place 40 days after the birth, provided she was well enough, when she would go to church to give thanks for her child. Today it is common for mothers, even first-time mothers, to be asked to leave their hospital beds only 24 hours or so after giving birth.

POST-NATAL DEPRESSION

Post-natal depression is not new. Indeed, it has probably always been present to some degree in almost every new mother – and no doubt the outside world has always failed to understand why, when both mother and child were alive and well, there should be any reason for despair instead of celebration.

"Occasional lowness and tendency to cry you must expect…it is what every lady suffers with more or less, and what I during my first two confinements suffered dreadfully with."
QUEEN VICTORIA TO HER DAUGHTER VICKY, 1859

FUTURE BIRTH CONTROL

Assuming she did not want a large family, the new mother's next concern was to make certain that in future her own or her partner's chosen form of contraceptive – whether sponge, condom (made from animal intestines) or *coitus interruptus* – was one that would work.

She might perhaps also have been worried by the superstitious belief that if a woman wants no more children she must keep the baby's cradle and some baby clothes in her home – and if she gives them away she will soon fall pregnant.

JUST AS HE THOUGHT HE HAD FINISHED.
TWO MORE !!!

2

THE NEW BABY

Although we are often told how much a *NEW BABY* learns in his first year and how rewarding he is, it can be the most tiring year for his mother. Try to relax and, if you can, work as little as possible – there's always the rest of your life. Be relaxed with your child, too. There is no need to push him to do things. Be patient, he will eventually do everything – in his own time.

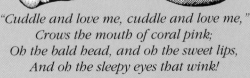

"Cuddle and love me, cuddle and love me,"
Crows the mouth of coral pink;
Oh the bald head, and oh the sweet lips,
And oh the sleepy eyes that wink!

From "I KNOW A BABY"
by CHRISTINA ROSSETTI (1830-94)

A GOOD START IN LIFE

A lifetime's bad luck
According to superstition, if a baby saw himself in a mirror before he was a year old he would have an unfortunate life. Consequently, in many households mirrors were not hung in the nursery.

Going up in the world
An older superstition decreed that when a child first left his mother's room he should go upstairs before he went downstairs or he would never rise in the world. Since the mother's room is often the highest in the house, parents were told that it would suffice if the nurse, holding the new baby, stepped up on a chair before leaving the room.

Bringing the baby home
Today some people consider it unlucky to bring a newborn baby home from hospital in the back seat of the car. (However, it may be safer than in the front.)

The first nappy
Before the disposable nappy was invented, it was considered unlucky to wash a baby's first nappy or to hang nappies out to dry by the light of the moon.

10946 Cupid Snap Waist for Children. Combination Hose Supporter, Waist and Shoulder Brace; no buttons, no button holes, no buckles. Everything goes on with a snap; can be removed or *put on* in a second's time.
Each........................$0.50
Postage.... .... .05
NOTE. If for girl send exact size of petticoat around the waist; for boy, size of kilts or pants around waist.

(Black only.)

The first outfit
In 1867 a learned journal noted that when an infant was first dressed his clothes should never be pulled on over his head (which would bring the child bad luck) but drawn on over his feet.

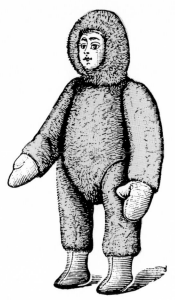

GETTING COLD FEET

In the seventeenth century, bachelor philosopher John Locke suggested that all children were molly-coddled and far too warmly dressed. He even told mothers to give their older children leaky shoes in order to get them used to having cold feet.

Today, the general rule is to dress your baby according to the weather, using as few clothes as possible, provided that he is cozy and warm enough. It doesn't matter if his hands and face feel a little bit cold – if his chest is warm, he will be too. Wool is generally used for the clothing of brand-new babies. Some children are allergic to it, but most are not. To stop him having a cold stomach, buy undershirts that fasten between the legs rather than ones that stop at the waist.

Always make sure that necklines are not too tight; and that any shawl your baby is given hasn't got large holes in which his fingers can get caught.

THE FIRST SMILE

You only see the first real smile once your child is six or seven weeks old – earlier "smiles" are thought to be grimaces due to wind. But once the baby does start smiling, gurgling, and eventually laughing you will no doubt find his infantile charms utterly beguiling.

"When the first baby laughed for the first time the laugh broke into a thousand pieces and they all went skipping about and that was the beginning of fairies."
J.M. BARRIE (1860-1937), author of PETER PAN

TOO TIGHT FOR COMFORT?

Up to the eighteenth century many mothers insisted on swaddling – wrapping the new baby up tightly. The baby Jesus was certainly dressed in swaddling clothes and for centuries some North-American Indian tribes bound their babies then strapped them to their mother's backs. Indeed, the word "papoose" was originally their word for baby, not for the pouchlike bag used for carrying the baby.

In 1762 the French philosopher Jean-Jacques Rousseau remonstrated with swaddling parents. Before birth, he argued, the baby is floating free and kicking in the womb, so why restrict his movements once he enters the world?

THE PURPOSE OF SWADDLING

The idea of swaddling was not to make the baby feel secure. It was meant to keep his limbs straight and help ward off rickets (a then rampant childhood disease), which of course it never did. Swaddling was regarded as important for the child "to give its little body a straight figure" and to "accustom him to keep upon his feet, who would otherwise go upon all fours, as most animals do." Sadly there were cases of babies dying from overheating, and sometimes the child's lungs were so constricted that he couldn't scream.

Luckily, these days any "swaddling" is just done with a shawl when the baby is put down to sleep, and his arms are usually left free.

HOW SWADDLING WAS DONE

Swaddling could take as much as two hours, which meant that the baby was fairly livid by the end of it – and probably so was the swaddler. The process consisted of wrapping the baby in a square of material around which long cloth strips, like bandages, were tightly wound – first around the baby's waist and then diagonally towards his feet and back up again. Once the bands had gone round the baby's chest, his arms were then bound to his trunk and wrapped in. To top it all, three cotton caps were put on his head in order to keep him warm.

CHANGING NAPPIES

Until the Victorian era when "towelling nappies" first appeared, nappies were usually linen and they weren't very absorbent. Around the same time, Mackintosh sheeting was invented. This was used for protecting the baby's mattress and it was also placed on the nurse's knee when changing the baby. However, babies' pants weren't made from Mackintosh, as it was feared that a "lazy nurse" might use them as an excuse for failing to change her charge.

Similarly, as late as the 1950s plastic pants were forbidden in some maternity hospitals on the grounds that they might give the illusion that the baby was permanently dry and therefore encourage an exhausted mother not to change her baby as often as she should.

THE DISPOSABLE NAPPY

The disposable nappy has been a merchandising coup of the last twenty years. You now buy them according to the sex and size of your child, rather than just one for all. They have their own little bags in which to dispose of them, and come with special baby-cleaning wipes to use with them. They have one disadvantage (besides preventing lazy mothers from realizing just how wet the baby is): if baby cream gets onto the fasteners, they won't stick together properly. In which case, the remedy is to use an old-fashioned nappy pin or a piece of masking tape to hold the nappy together.

Nursery Rubber Sheeting.

IN WHITE ONLY.

14071 Width	27 in.	36 in.	45 in.	54 in.
Price, per yard	40c.	60c.	75c.	$0.95
Weight, per yard	15 oz.	18 oz.	22 oz.	28 oz.

Diapers.

14073 Rubber Diaper Drawers. Come in 3 sizes –small medium and large.
Each.....................$0.25
Per dozen..............2.75
Diaper weighs 6 ounces.

WHEN TO CHANGE

A very new baby only needs to have his nappy changed at mealtimes. But don't change him if he is starving hungry – let him feed first and then change him afterwards. Only if he isn't ravenous should you change him first.

A crying baby does not usually signify a dirty nappy Until a baby is at least six months old, having a dirty nappy won't bother him in the least.

If your baby's bed is wet in the morning, that means his nappy isn't large enough. Increase its capacity by putting a nappy pad (similar to a sanitary napkin) inside the nappy to absorb the urine.

RASH REMEDIES

Today zinc-and-castor-oil cream is used on the baby's bottom to prevent nappy rash. Before its invention, capon grease or vegetable oil were used.

If your baby has a nappy rash, try these hints to help it go away:

- Change his nappies frequently.
- Use old-fashioned towelling nappies, instead of disposable ones, and leave off the plastic pants.
- Clean the rash carefully at each change with warm olive oil, rather than soap and water or baby wipes, and spread a thick layer of zinc-and-castor-oil cream over the rash before putting on a new nappy.
- Or try covering the rash with a beaten egg white. It quickly forms a thin skin over the rash that provides some degree of protection while it heals.
- Exposing the rash to air for as long periods as possible is the surest way to heal it. Place a sanitary towel or similar pad over your boy's penis and under your girl's bottom to soak up the urine while they are not wearing a nappy.

If the rash doesn't go away after a few days, report it to your doctor.

IMBIBED WITH MOTHER'S MILK

It was once thought that human milk was "white blood". The theory was put forward by Galen, the second-century Greek physician, who suggested that menstruation stopped when a woman got pregnant because the blood was channelled to feed the foetus. Once the baby was born, the blood went to her breasts instead, where it emerged white and nourishing. He believed that just as the mother imparted some of her personality to the child at conception, so she would continue to develop and enrich his personality at the breast.

TEA STRAINERS FOR SORE NIPPLES

Whether the mother begins feeding her baby immediately after birth or 24 hours later doesn't matter, the baby will not mind provided he is given a little boiled water. However, it's best to start breast-feeding gradually, or you will find that your nipples become very sore. Begin with a few minutes at each feed. Then build up minute by minute over a week or so to 20 minutes per feed, with 10 minutes at each breast (or 20 minutes at one breast, alternating every feed).

While pregnant, never use soap on your nipples. After washing them, just with hot water, splash cold water over your breasts to close the pores. Until a few years ago, when a chamomile cream took over in popularity, nursing mothers rubbed friar's balsam on their nipples between feeds. Exposing your nipples to the air is the best cure for sore breasts. Place a tea strainer over each of your nipples and wear your bra on top – this allows the air to get to them.

SWEET AND SOUR BREASTS

A delightful belief that lingered into modern times was that one breast supplied sweet milk while the other was savoury. Swapping breasts half way through a feed therefore gave the baby the best of both worlds.

INJUDICIOUS FEEDING

"It is improper and pernicious to keep infants continually at the breast; and it would be less hurtful, nay, even judicious, to let them cry for a few nights, rather than to fill them incessantly with milk, which weakens the digestive organs, and ultimately generates scrofulous affections."

From ENQUIRE WITHIN UPON EVERYTHING, 1877

ACQUIRED TASTES

When breast-feeding, spicy foods should be excluded from your diet – as they are in the East – and mainly boiled and steamed foods eaten. Cucumber and fried meat were once thought of as giving the baby colic. Other mothers find their babies are affected when they eat cauliflower, cabbage, lentils or other wind-inducing foods. Strawberries seem to be an almost universally forbidden fruit, but some babies obligingly don't notice if the mother is tempted.

In the past, wet nurses were always told to abstain from any medicines, as they would appear in the milk and affect the baby. However, use was made of this route if the baby needed medicine (if you're thinking of doing this, it is vital to check with your doctor first).

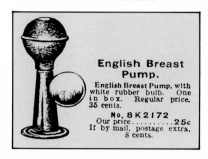

English Breast Pump.

English Breast Pump, with white rubber bulb. One in box. Regular price, 35 cents.

No. 8 K 2 1 7 2
Our price.........25c
If by mail, postage extra, 8 cents.

STIMULATING PRODUCTION

In the sixteenth century Omnibonus Ferrarius invented a breast pump to stimulate milk production. This worked by the mother sucking one end – then, once the milk started flowing, the pump was removed and the child placed on the breast instead.

USING A WET NURSE

Until the nineteenth century, when sterilization was understood and bottles could be safely used, babies that were not breast-fed rarely survived. Breast-feeding was not an option but a must – although the breast did not necessarily have to be the mother's.

Throughout the centuries there have been many mothers that either couldn't or didn't want to feed their new baby. As early as the second century the Greek physician Galen advised breast-feeding mothers to abstain from sex since intercourse curdled the milk. No doubt husbands who wanted to resume sexual relations with their wives as quickly as possible, either for enjoyment or to produce a male heir, made sure there was a wet nurse available before too long.

Wet nurses were often highly respectable women who took in suckling babies to supplement their husband's income. They would nurse the children in their own homes, only returning them to their parents when they were weaned. In 1662 a well-to-do English mother, the Countess of Lincoln, wrote a book in praise of mothers feeding their children themselves, since she had sent all eighteen of her own children away to be nursed and only one of them had survived.

THE PLEASURES OF FEEDING

In the sixteenth century a French doctor asked his women patients if they considered their breasts to be merely decorative. He suggested to them that if they knew the erotic pleasure that could be derived from breast-feeding they wouldn't be in such a hurry to hand their children over to wet nurses.

STEMMING THE FLOW

It was widely believed that, once the child had been given to the wet nurse, if the mother put on her husband's shirt that would stop her own milk coming.

THE OTHER OPTION

"Cow's milk, diluted with water until it is brought to the same consistency as mother's milk, unmixed either with flour, bread, biscuit or sugar, is by far the best substitute...In hot weather the milk should be fresh drawn at least once in eight hours, and never given warmer than it comes from the cow...This method is undoubtedly preferable to the bare hazard of imbibing ill-humour, or disease, from a woman whose temper and constitution must be very imperfectly known."

LADY SARAH PENNINGTON, 1760

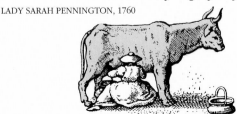

STRAIGHT FROM THE BEAST

Although animal milk was obviously a possible substitute for human milk, there was always the problem of how to get it into the child's mouth. The story of Romulus and Remus popularized the wolf as mother, and as late as 1896 childcare manuals were recommending that babies should be fed directly from the animal as the milk would be both fresh and clean.

Goats and donkeys were regarded as the ideal source of supply, because their milk had the smallest curds, but cow's milk was generally easier to obtain.

"Each goat which comes to feed, enters bleating into the ward, and goes to hunt the infant which has been given to it, pushes back the covering with its horns, and straddles the crib to give suck to the infant."

ALPHONSE LE ROY, DESCRIBING A FRENCH FOUNDLING INSTITUTION, 1775

WEANING WISDOM

Every mother probably feels hesitant as she begins to wean her child. It is the beginning of the next stage of his life, the start of his life without her. It is a new situation for both, and the mother cannot be sure how her child will react. In the past, weaning was a particularly worrying time as the baby would no longer be receiving the immunity to diseases that his mother's milk gave him.

Today most children are given their first food when four months old. In the second century, the Greek physician Galen had suggested that the arrival of the first tooth signalled the child was ready to begin solid food – and modern medicine concurs that this is the time when mothers should start weaning. Galen also decreed that it was best to continue breast-feeding till the baby's last milk teeth erupted.

The exact day to start weaning had to be chosen extremely carefully, and there was much superstition surrounding the best day to start:

A propitious beginning
The ideal time to begin weaning was on a holy day or day of good omen (preferably Good Friday) or on a full moon (the following waning moon would help a mother reduce her flow of milk).

Dates to avoid
The least auspicious time to begin was on any Friday (since Fridays in general, except for Good Friday, were regarded as unlucky); or December 28th (Childermas, which commemorated the massacre of the children ordered by King Herod and was therefore considered the unluckiest day of the year for anything to do with children); or any time when the birds were migrating (since the child would grow up restless).

Finishing in time
The ideal time to finish weaning was in the spring rather than the winter (when there was plenty of fresh food around); or in the fall (when the risk of summer diarrhoea was over).

THE FIRST FEEDING BOTTLES

The artificial nipple as we know it was invented in 1845, but the ancient Romans had both pottery and glass feeding bottles. In medieval times cows' horns were sometimes used as feeding bottles with the addition of a sewn parchment or soft-leather nipple, the milk flowing through the stitches. These had the virtue of being easy to make. Moreover, the milk could be topped up from above and, since a horn couldn't readily be stood on end, the milk would usually be drunk at once and not left to go sour. However, such containers were clearly unhygienic.

"I have often thought that a round flexible pipe might be contrived, full of small holes at the end, within which pipe a piece of sponge might be placed to stop the liquor from flowing out, unless pressed or drawn by suction, and this pipe screwed to a spout on the vessel which contains the liquor... such a pipe might remain in their mouths until they dropped asleep, or took their heads from it."

LADY SARAH PENNINGTON, 1760

LET THEM DRINK ALCOHOL

In the days when it was common for water supplies to be dangerously contaminated, once weaned from the breast children would often be given beer or wine to drink instead:

"Breakfast for the Nursery, for my Lady Margaret and Mr Ingram Percy, a manchet [fine bread], one quart of beer, 3 mutton bones boiled."

FROM THE EARL OF NORTHUMBERLAND'S HOUSEHOLD ACCOUNTS, 1512

LADY MARGARET AND INGRAM were just three years old and eighteen months, respectively.

RELIEF FROM FLATULENCE

"If the babe should suffer [wind], a little dill or aniseed may be added to the food – half a teaspoon of dill water... Warm olive oil, well rubbed, for a quarter of an hour at a time, by means of the warm hand, over the bowels, will frequently give relief. Turning the child over on his bowels, so that they may press on the nurse's lap, will often afford great comfort. A warm bath (where he is suffering severely) generally gives immediate ease in flatulence...

Hiccough may generally be traced to over-feeding. Should it be severe, four or five grains of calcined magnesia, with a little syrup and aniseed water, and attention to feeding, are all that will be necessary."

From ADVICE TO A MOTHER by PYE HENRY CHAVASSE, c.1914

Where 'ere you be
Let your wind go free
TRADITIONAL RHYME

SUGAR WATER AND FLOWERS FOR DIARRHOEA

The first thing to do if your new baby gets diarrhoea is to stop giving him milk, and give him a solution of 1¾ pints of boiled water mixed with 8 tablespoons of sugar and 1 teaspoon of salt to sip slowly instead.

In the seventeenth century children frequently died from summer diarrhoea. One remedy for it was a brew of diascordion (either dissolved in a syrup of red poppies or gillyflowers or put into a conserve of roses to cover the taste) and then a little syrup before bed.

DIASCORDION A medicine made of the dried leaves of a strongly scented plant called *Teucrium scordium* and many other herbs.

GILLYFLOWERS Clove-scented carnations or other similarly scented plants, such as wall-flowers or white stocks.

FIRST STEPS

In the seventeenth century there were conflicting opinions as to when a baby should take his first steps.

François Mauriceau told mothers that crawling was animal-like – so they should stop their children from crawling lest bestial behaviour become a characteristic of their adult life.

The philosopher John Locke, on the other hand, after a visit to the New World, told of babies allowed to scrabble about like kittens who not only walked earlier than European babies but were just as strong as adults and not at all bestial.

THE VIRTUE OF NIGHTSHIRTS

If your child is wearing a nightshirt, it is very easy to change his nappy: you just lift it up, there are no press studs, and no pulling in and out of tight legs. In a nightshirt the baby can also play with the hem – it's a sort of built-in toy – and the air can get to his legs.

If he wears an all-in-one stretchsuit, make sure the legs and feet aren't too short or tight (if they are, you can always cut them off at the ankles).

There is no need for your child to have different outfits for day and night until he is a few months old, unless you want to show him off to family and friends.

3

SWEET DREAMS

No matter how much a mother loves her child, there is always a time she needs to set aside for herself, and that is usually those precious moments when her child is asleep and sweetly dreaming. A baby needs his *SLEEPING TIME* too – a time alone, to grow and digest, and for comfort and healing.

There never was a child so lovely but that his mother was glad to get him asleep.

RALPH WALDO EMERSON (1803-82)

A SOFA FOR NANNY

"Your nursery should be light and roomy, with a window opening top and bottom. Make it cheerful and pretty, wallpapers pale blue or pink...Don't be afraid of furniture that might seem strange to the nursery. A huge sofa is a god-send to a tired Nanny – and the children can use it as a ship!"

From FROM KITCHEN TO GARRET : HINTS FOR YOUNG HOUSEHOLDERS, 1888

THE IDEAL ENVIRONMENT

Views have varied a lot as to the temperature of the room the child should sleep in.

A hundred years ago, some authorities maintained that the windows should never be opened at night but might be left open all day long in fine weather. It was also considered important that the room, as well as being lofty, dry and spacious, should not be inhabited during the day. It was recommended that no linen or washed clothes be hung in the room to dry, as that would contaminate the air.

By the 1920s pure fresh air was thought of as having healing qualities that even the sickliest child would benefit from. Ventilation was now considered essential. It was suggested that the window should be opened at least two inches, and only be closed while the baby was being changed or bathed or when there was fog.

The windows opened more
would keep doctors from the door.
TRADITIONAL RHYME

THE DANGERS OF SMOTHERING

In the ninth century the Church condemned the then common practice of a baby sleeping in the bed of his parents or wet nurse and advised that children should sleep alone in their cradles until they were three years old. It was thought that many babies were accidentally smothered by the sleeping adult.

In Victorian times parents were still being warned about the risk of smothering small children. However, recent studies have shown that provided the baby can move there is little danger of suffocation – and since swaddling is no longer used, there would seem to be no reason for the baby getting trapped.

CRADLES WITHOUT FRILLS

"The sensible up-to-date mother does without billows of frills and laces, and bunches made up of innumerable yards of ribbon. She considers health and utility first."
From THE BOOK OF THE HOME, 1922

A BED OF HIS OWN?

Since it is the mother who is most likely to lack sleep during the first year or two after childbirth, and rarely the baby, sleeping arrangements should be geared to suit her. If you enjoy suckling your child until you both fall asleep next to each other in bed, there is no need to have fears or inhibitions about doing so. On the other hand, if the baby's snufflings and gurglings keep you awake, don't feel guilty about putting him somewhere close enough for you to hear his cries but far enough away for each little wriggle and intake of breath not to wake you up.

WHAT KIND OF BED?

Babies have on occasion slept in all sorts of places – in an empty drawer, taken from a chest of drawers, or a clothes basket or even a cardboard box. In India, babies are placed in cradles that hang from the ceiling on chains to prevent rats climbing over them. In the West, cradles have traditionally been raised from the ground so that the occupant would be away from floor-level draughts.

Today parents tend to move children from a cradle into a crib once they are about six months old and from a crib into a bed when they are about two. But a crib is so secure and cozy; the child can rest books or toys against the rails; and you can always leave the side down once he is old enough to hop out to go to the bathroom. So don't be in too much of a hurry to move him. Why force him to grow up?

SOFT LANDING

When your child eventually moves from a cot to a bed, place the mattress of the cot on the floor next to him – then if he falls out, he won't get such a shock.

SLEEP ON IT

Feather mattresses and pillows were banished from nurseries in the nineteenth century as they were thought to be debilitating – no doubt because some children were allergic to the feathers. Hair mattresses were regarded as the best, although they were the most expensive.

As recently as the 1940s some parents in rural areas were still making mattresses for their children – with cases of unbleached calico and fillings of cut chaff, which they got from the local miller or grain store. The chaff was heated in the oven or turned over in the sun to sterilize it, then it was carefully sorted to remove prickly ends.

TO REST HIS HEAD

In the past, horsehair pillows were given to very young babies, as it was thought that if the pillow was firm enough the child would not be able to bury his nose in it. Today, it is considered unwise to give a child who is less than one year old any kind of pillow because of the risk of smothering.

WHAT TIME BEDTIME?

In the 1920s the fashion was for putting children to bed at 6 p.m. It was thought that keeping a child up in the evening would lead to wakeful nights and make the child nervous and irritable. Today small children are often allowed to stay up later in the evenings, and are also expected to sleep later in the mornings. We are no longer as guided by the sun as we were.

Children invariably seem to think of going to bed as something that they don't want to do, rather than as a pleasure or a treat at the end of a long day. But bed should never be thought of as a punishment, or as a cutting off point. It should be presented to children as just another part of the day, a very special part. So don't threaten your child with bed – instead, make bed seem enticing.

Go to bed late,
Stay very small;
Go to bed early,
Grow very tall.
NURSERY RHYME

FLEURS DU MAL

"Plants and flowers ought not to be allowed to remain in a chamber at night. Experiments have proved that plants and flowers take up, in the daytime, carbonic-acid gas (the refuse of respiration), and give off oxygen (a gas so necessary and beneficial to health), but give out, in the night season, a poisonous exhalation."
From ADVICE TO A MOTHER by PYE HENRY CHAVASSE, c.1914

FACING BOTH WAYS

There are conflicting superstitions about the direction a sleeping child (or adult) should lie in. Some believe that a bed should point east/west, and that if it points north/south the sleeper will have nightmares. Others believe that a north/south alignment aids a peaceful night and deep sleep.

SLEEPING BY NUMBERS

- *At 1 month your baby needs 21 hours sleep*
- *At 6 months your baby needs 18 hours sleep*
- *At 1 year your baby needs 15 hours sleep*
- *At 4 years your baby needs 13 hours sleep*
- *At 6 years your baby needs 12 hours sleep*
- *At 9 years your child needs 11 hours sleep*

Adapted from THE MOTHERCRAFT MANUAL by MABEL LIDDIARD, 1923

WHY DOESN'T MY BABY SLEEP?

Babies are all born different. Some are born placid and contented – babies that fit in with any reasonable routine and are good sleepers. Others are more temperamental and need less sleep. Mothers are also all different. Some provide a feeling of security and tranquillity conducive to sleep. Others, who pick their babies up frequently for a cuddle or a chat, may find that a more peaceful, undisturbed atmosphere inspires a longer sleep.

GENTLE STROKING

It is said that some nannies masturbated their charges, aged two or three, with their hands to soothe them to sleep – and that in India ayahs did it with their toes.

BEDTIME FROLICS

Children need to know what their day holds in store for them and they need a calm bedtime. Often a working parent arrives home just in time to join in bathing the baby. This generates an overdose of excitement, rather than a peaceful bedtime atmosphere. One solution is for the parent to spend time with the child early in the morning (perhaps have a bath together then) rather than last thing at night.

WHY IS HE WAKEFUL?

If your baby cries in the night, go through this little checklist in your mind. Once you have reassured yourself that there's no alarming reason for him to cry, you can put him back to bed with a clear conscience. Never leave a baby crying for a long time, especially a new baby. Crying is his only way of communicating.

- *Is he hungry? Or thirsty?*
- *Is he ill?*
- *Is there a nappy pin sticking into him?*
- *Is he too hot or too cold?*
- *Is he having a nightmare, or just feeling troubled?*

DESPERATE MEASURES

Babies that won't sleep are not a new problem. In the eighteenth and nineteenth centuries fretful babies were often given a dose of opium. This sometimes led to the death of the child since harassed or lazy mothers and nurses preferred a peaceful if drugged baby to a wakeful one, regardless of the consequences.

The opium was either given direct to the child or smeared around the mother's (or wet nurse's) nipple for the baby to suck. It was also believed then, as now, that if the feeding mother drank a little alcohol before the night-time feed it might travel through her into her child's stomach and give both of them a quiet night – a practice not to be recommended.

Hush-a-bye, baby, on tree top,
When the wind blows the cradle will rock;
When the bough breaks the cradle will fall,
Down will come baby, cradle, and all.

NURSERY RHYME

ROCKING YOUR BABY TO SLEEP

The late eighteenth century saw the design of the first cradle to stand firmly on four legs. Before that, cradles were mounted on rockers, and the swaddled baby had to be strapped in so he wouldn't get tipped out onto the floor. Nevertheless, rocking cradles remained popular and Thomas Sheraton, the British cabinet maker, designed an automatically rocking cradle with a clock mechanism that swung steadily to and fro, like a pendulum, for twenty minutes or more.

ADDICTIVE ROCKING

"Cots on rockers should not be used. Apart from the fact that inducing sleep by a rocking motion becomes a bad habit and spoils the child, the motion is very unhealthy. A baby's brain is exceedingly delicate, and the rocking or jolting motion is very harmful indeed for the tiny organism, and may even be the cause of future mental or nervous disorders."

From THE BOOK OF THE HOME, 1922

BEDWETTING

It seems bedwetting has long been a worry to parents since so many "remedies" for it have been devised. Nowadays it is suggested that the best remedy for bedwetting is to ignore it, as it will usually cease of its own accord once the child is older (although he may well be in his teens before it stops altogether).

The typical bedwetter is probably slightly tense or nervous during the day and only relaxes when asleep. The best approach is therefore to find out why he is anxious during waking hours and remove the cause, rather than focus attention on the problem by trying to "cure" it, thus causing the child additional anxiety.

Country cure
In nineteenth-century rural England a bedwetting child would be sent out to search for an ash tree and gather the "keys" (seeds) from it. He would have to place them with his left hand in the crook of his right arm and then walk home. At home the keys would be placed in the fire and burnt and the child would urinate on them, at which moment he would be cured.

Gentle cure
One suggested cure was to sponge the "lower parts" of the body morning and evening with tepid water.

Abrasive cure
Another traditional remedy was to give a bedwetter a concoction of eggshells ground in milk or water to eat.

Magic cure
An occult cure for bedwetting was to get the child to urinate on the grave of a child of the opposite sex.

Aversion therapy
Not so long ago, in certain areas bedwetters were fed on a regular diet of mice.

WAKING UP

No doubt the grogginess many adults experience on waking may help them understand that children can feel similarly muzzy. A Victorian household manual explained to inconsiderate parents that:

"To awaken children from their sleep with a noise, or in an impetuous manner, is extremely injudicious and hurtful; nor is it proper to carry them from a dark room immediately into a glaring light, or against a dazzling wall; for the sudden impression of light debilitates the organs of vision, and lays the foundation of weak eyes from early infancy."

From ENQUIRE WITHIN UPON EVERYTHING, 1877

The cock doth crow
To let you know
If you be wise
'Tis time to rise:
For early to bed,
And early to rise,
Is the way to be healthy
And wealthy and wise.

NURSERY RHYME

DANGER AT THE BOTTOM OF THE BED

Children have been known to suffocate because the blankets at the bottom of the bed were tucked in. They have snuggled down the bed during the night and not been able to breathe. Never tuck in the blankets at the foot of a child's bed.

SLEEPING OUTSIDE

For years it was the fashion for a mother, during fine weather, to leave her baby outside in the garden or on the balcony to sleep for much of the day. She would put him in a large, deep pram – shaded from the sun and away from insects in summer, and out of the wind and well wrapped up against cold in winter. It was an excellent idea, as the baby could lie there peacefully staring up at the trees or watching the clouds go by, getting plenty of fresh air.

BUZZZZZZZZ

There is an old belief that if a bee flies round a child when he is asleep it means he will have a happy life.

4

HUNGRY TUMMIES

Often far too much fuss is made over what children eat and what they don't. Children are intuitively aware of which foods their bodies require in order to grow and flourish, and they can usually be left to decide what their needs are. Neither ask them what they want to eat nor worry if they skip a meal. Just present them with a well-balanced diet and let them judge for themselves how much *FOOD* their body needs at a particular moment.

Children and chicken
Must always be pickin'
TRADITIONAL RHYME

FIRST FOOD

The usual practice today is to place the newborn baby on the mother's breast immediately to let his sucking instinct be rewarded. However, until modern times new babies were given nothing but water for the first 24 hours after birth.

In the more distant past, the significance of the first nourishment of life was considered crucial and there were many superstitions regarding the first thing that should cross the newborn baby's lips. Nowadays some of these substances would not be given to a child before he is ready for solids, if at all.

English babies
In some parts of England restless babies used to be given a little jelly made from hare's brains to quiet them. In other parts a new baby would be given a drink of water into which a red-hot cinder had been dropped. The cinder was a symbol of life-giving fire and was supposed to bring good health to the baby.

Scottish babies
Babies born in autumn were sometimes given the "milk" of the hazelnut as their first food. It was hoped that this would bring good luck and health. If the child did not flourish, he would later be fed with further doses of hazelnut milk, this time mixed with honey.

Welsh babies
The attributes of the bee were considered so magical that honey mixed with butter was often given immediately after birth to the new baby. It was believed that some of the powers and sweetness of the bee would be passed on to the baby. If honey was not available, moist sugar was substituted.

Nordic babies
Among pagan Norsemen it was common to smear honey on the tip of the father's sword and feed it to a boy baby so he would grow up to be a strong fighter.

FIRST DRINK

Instead of giving the newborn child special food, for the first few days after childbirth the ancient Aztecs provided the mother with an alcoholic drink called octli that was thought to have a tonic effect. Octli was made from the fermented sap of the multi-purpose maguey cactus and was so strong that the mother was allowed only two goblets. A drink akin to octli, named pulque, is still available in Mexico today.

STARTING SOLIDS

The very first solid food a baby usually eats these days is a boiled and puréed carrot and some cereal at around four months. A week or two later he will be eating mashed bananas and other cooked and puréed fruit and vegetables. About a month later he will savour his first boiled-egg yolk, yogurt, and a little cooked chicken and fish. As most children enjoy the sensation of feeling a bone on their new teeth, he will some-times be handed a chicken or lamb bone to gnaw on, which will act as a teething ring as well as providing a bit of nourishment.

THE VIRTUES OF CHEWING

"Proper mastication is necessary for the development of the jaws... Narrow jaws and want of width of the palate leads to a narrow nasal cavity, want of room in the nose, to mouth breathing and adenoids. Hence the importance of hard foods rather than the soft mushy substances usually prepared for children."
From THE MOTHERCRAFT MANUAL by MABEL LIDDIARD, 1923

BLENDERS ANCIENT AND MODERN

A medieval writer noted that the duties of a wet nurse included chewing a piece of bread until her saliva softened it, then rolling it into a ball and giving it to the baby to eat. She treated meat and vegetables the same way, using her teeth as a blade.

Nowadays catering for small children is so much easier – and much more hygienic. One invaluable time-saving idea is to cook and purée a carrot, potato or apple, or any food you happen to be eating (provided it is not spiced), then freeze it in an ice-cube tray. When an instant meal is needed, one ice-cube portion of thoroughly re-heated food is usually sufficient for one small infant.

FISH AT FIRST

Fish can be given to children over six months of age. Start with plaice and sole and only give the baby coarser fish, such as cod and unsmoked haddock, once they are a little older. Oily fish such as mackerel and trout should not be given until the child is over a year old. Shellfish should never be given to children at all, as it can produce serious allergies.

Fish is good for the brain.
TRADITIONAL SAYING

NO MEAT ON THE MENU

Today it is known that a normal baby has enough iron already in his liver for it not to be necessary for him to be fed meat until he is six months old. Most meats are then suitable for the baby, with the exception of ham and bacon (which should wait until he is ten months old) and pork (which should only be given to him after his second birthday as it's very difficult to digest).

In the 1920s a manual advised mothers not to serve their children meat until they were twelve months old. The author gave three reasons:

- *Meat is acid-forming.*
- *The protein in it is more susceptible to putrefaction in the intestines than the protein in milk, fish, eggs, and selected vegetables, which are more easily digested.*
- *It is too stimulating for nervous children.*

FOOD TABOOS

The list of foods forbidden to children in the 1930s would bear very little resemblance to any such list compiled today. At that time hard-boiled eggs, cheese, tinned and salted foods, duck, goose, ham, pastry, pickles, radishes, turnips, cucumber, mushrooms, herring, mackerel, crabs, currants, raisins and nuts were all to be excluded from the child's diet. No food was to be fried, sweets were not to be given, and no stimulants (including tea or coffee) were to be drunk unless prescribed by a doctor.

It is interesting to note that even in the Orient, where spicy foods are part of the staple diet, a child is not usually fed spices until he is two years old.

FRUIT AND VEGETABLES

Cucumber is still considered indigestible and should not be given to children under two. Onions and leeks are also difficult for a child to digest and tend to cause flatulence, so omit them from your child's diet for the first twelve months. Sweet corn and currants pass straight through the child's system whole until the child is about three and so need not be given until then. Strawberries and raspberries should be sieved when given to a child under twelve months old.

HEAVY ON THE TUMMY

Today, cheese and unripe bananas are often singled out as being particularly indigestible and likely to give a child nightmares. In fact, it's best to avoid giving a child anything heavy to eat close to bedtime.

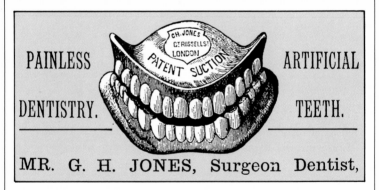

PAINLESS DENTISTRY.

CH. JONES
C? RUSSELLS?
LONDON
PATENT SUCTION

ARTIFICIAL TEETH.

MR. G. H. JONES, Surgeon Dentist,

BAD FOR THEIR TEETH

Nowadays, dentists are becoming increasingly concerned about the fruit-drinks craze. When fruit is eaten raw or cooked, the mouth produces saliva which partially cleans the teeth and gums. With fruit drinks, no saliva is produced and so the acidity of the fruit remains on the child's teeth until brushed off. Give your child water instead of fruit drinks, or make sure he brushes his teeth after drinking them. Never put fruit drinks in a baby's bottle.

FORBIDDEN FRUIT

To medieval minds the maggots seen in fruit and vegetables so resembled the threadworms commonly found in children that the fruit and vegetables were wrongly thought of as being the source. All fruit and vegetables were therefore thoroughly boiled before they were given to children – which killed not only the maggots but the vitamins too.

At the same time, medieval medical thinking maintained that fresh fruit was harmful to babies and young children, so it was forbidden to them. This prohibition led to deficiency of Vitamin C. As a result, many growing children developed scurvy. The prevailing wisdom was that scurvy was either caused by too much salt in the diet (which led to children being forbidden salt) or contracted through kissing infected parents (which no doubt led to some strained family relations). It was not until the mid eighteenth century that scurvy was eventually linked with lack of Vitamin C.

Ap-ple.

DEVELOPING THEIR TASTE BUDS

Children are often fussy about food, but childish likes and dislikes are not the same the world over. In North America and Britain children are expected to like sweet things and turn up their noses at anything that is savoury – but most Belgian children dislike puddings, and North African children delight in chewing raw red peppers. In Mexico the traditional daily ration was half a tortilla for a three-year-old and two tortillas per day for a boy aged thirteen.

Wilful waste brings woeful want
And you may live to say,
How I wish I had that crust
That once I threw away.
NURSERY RHYME

NEITHER COAX NOR TEMPT

"If a child refuse his food, neither coax nor tempt him to eat… Depend on it, there is always a cause for a want of appetite: perhaps his stomach has been over-worked and requires repose; or his bowels are loaded, and Nature wishes to take time to use up the old material… Kind Nature, if we will but listen to her voice, will tell us when to eat and when to refrain."

From ADVICE TO A MOTHER by PYE HENRY CHAVASSE, c.1914

WEIGHTY CONSIDERATIONS

A standard birth weight is around 7 pounds. For the first few days the newborn baby will lose weight. Then he will start gaining, at the rate of about an ounce a day. After the first month he will have gained at least a pound. By the second month the average baby weighs 11 pounds. By five months most babies have doubled their birth weight, and by a year they should weigh three times their birth weight or more.

Until quite recently it was considered unlucky to weigh a baby before he was one year old – a weighed child, it was believed, would probably not thrive. As late as 1935 a British woman refused to have her baby weighed on the grounds that her elder child, who was mentally retarded, had been weighed when small and that was why he "went funny"

Your eyes are bigger than your belly.

TRADITIONAL SAYING

MANNERS MAKETH MAN

The best way for a child to learn table manners is by example. If parents eat in a civilized fashion, then their children will eventually eat in a civilized fashion too. Some manners are just plain politeness, others were designed to aid digestion or prevent accidents at table.

Politeness
Refraining from talking with a full mouth spares diners opposite an unsightly view and reduces the likelihood of choking. Eating at roughly the same pace (be it fast or slow) as fellow diners avoids the embarrassment of anyone finishing first or last.

Aids to digestion
Taking only one sandwich at a time from a platter and placing it on your own plate before eating it is to stop food being crammed into the mouth. It also ensures that those whose eyes are bigger than their belly don't grab more than they can eat.

Only eating desserts and cakes after savoury foods is to make sure a child doesn't fill up on sweet things and ruin his appetite for the vitamins and proteins.

Safety manners
The point of tilting a soup bowl away from you is to prevent scalding-hot soup spilling from the bowl into your lap as you spoon the soup to your mouth.

Keeping your elbows off the table, and your hands on your lap once you've finished eating, saves glasses and other items on the table from being knocked over.

Slippery manners
In the 1920s there was one infallible clue to a child's social background. If he ate his jelly with a fork, you knew he was well brought up.

Of a little take a little,
You're kindly welcome, too;
Of a little leave a little,
'Tis manners so to do.
NURSERY RHYME

DRINKING DURING MEALS

"Many children acquire a habit of drinking during their meals; it would be more conducive to digestion if they were accustomed to drink only after having made a meal."

From ENQUIRE WITHIN UPON EVERYTHING, 1877

I'M NOT HUNGRY!

Never force a child to eat his food or bring the same plate back meal after meal until its contents have been eaten. If you find you're upset at your child constantly failing to eat meals you have laboured to prepare, go out and buy some instant meals for him. He may even surprise you by eating them up.

If you display too much concern about your child's diet, you may succeed in increasing his finickiness or reluctance to eat. On the other hand, it is a good idea to give children (even those with healthy appetites) supplementary multi-vitamin pills, especially in winter.

5

NOT BY SOAP ALONE

Even in the earlier part of this century the chances of a baby surviving to adolescence were quite small. This statistic placed an entirely different emphasis on child rearing. Today many of the worries of motherhood are psychological, whereas in the past they were almost entirely concerned with the child's physical *WELL-BEING*. How to keep the baby alive and healthy was a very real, and sometimes overwhelming, worry.

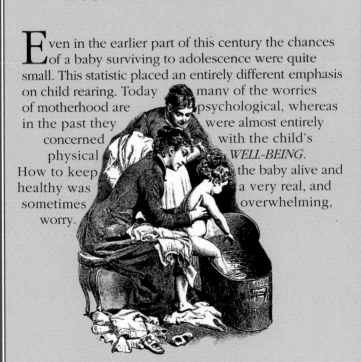

*On Saturday night shall be my care
To powder my locks and curl my hair.*
NURSERY RHYME

AT THE SEA-SIDE.
PUZZLE:-FIND PORTRAITS OF THE CHILDREN'S PARENTS.

THE HEALING SUN

In 1612 a Frenchman, Jacques Guillemeau, advised mothers and nurses to take the baby outside for part of the day. However, it wasn't until the late eighteenth century that mothers were convinced that exposure to the sun was beneficial to the child.

In the Orient first thing in the morning, when the sun is already bright but not yet too hot, new babies are commonly given a full body and head massage in the open, using olive oil as a lubricant. This daily dose of sunshine provides a valuable source of Vitamin D, while the massage tones up the child's muscles.

At the turn of this century there were differing views as to how many minutes a day a baby should spend in the sun. Some considered five minutes enough for a newborn baby, building up to ten minutes at three months; others thought twenty minutes preferable. All agreed that veils should never be used, as they prevented the intake of fresh air and the escape of the "poisoned" exhaled breath. It was thought sufficient if dusty streets were avoided and a sunshade used.

CLEANLINESS IS NEXT TO GODLINESS

Children love baths and find water play extremely therapeutic. For a safe and happy bathtime:

- Don't use a lot of soap or bubble bath, as both can remove useful oils from the skin.
- Don't fill the tub up to the brim (a few inches is all a child needs).
- Placing a wash cloth over a hot tap or pipe is likely to draw a child's attention to it. Instead, turn the temperature of the hot water down, so the child cannot burn or scald himself.
- It is essential to stay with a child all the time he is in the bath. So gather up everything you need beforehand; unplug the telephone or turn on your answering machine; and pin a note on the front door if you are expecting visitors or a delivery. Never leave your child alone in the bath – even for a few seconds. A baby can drown in a few inches of water.
- Install a mirror in your bathroom at child height, so your child can be involved in his bathtime routine.

THE VIRTUES OF A COLD RINSE

Rinsing with cold water after a hot wash closes the pores in the skin and boosts circulation. It is not a bad idea to get children used to cold water as well as hot. Massaging babies after bathing also encourages the circulation and was recommended to mothers in a manual at the turn of the century. Parts that ought to be especially well rubbed, the book suggested, were "the back, the chest, the limbs and the bowels."

POURING OIL ON WATER

If your child has dry skin, a few drops of baby oil in the bath will help get rid of the dryness and will be beneficial for your hands, too. But take extra care – oil makes the bath, and the child, slippery.

RICH TRIMMINGS

If you want your child's hair to grow thickly or quickly, it should be cut when the moon is waxing. If you want it to stay short, cut it when the moon is on the wane. Mondays, Tuesdays and Wednesdays were traditionally the best days of the week for a trim, since according to folklore a person who cut hair on other days would never get rich.

GOGGLE-EYED

After their first year children often rebel against having their hair washed. The simplest thing is just to get on with it as calmly and as quickly as you can; but if you think it would make your child happier, equip him with swimming goggles so he won't get shampoo in his eyes. When you have finished washing your child's hair, it's a good move to cut it while he's still in the bath – he will probably be quite happy to go on playing while his hair is being trimmed.

SOME STICKY SITUATIONS

There are some delightfully simple solutions to many of the most common haircare problems:

Removing chewing gum
Hold an ice cube against the chewing gum to freeze it solid, then peel the gum out of the hair; or loosen the gum with peanut butter.

Curing dandruff
Washing a child's hair with whipped egg yolk is a traditional cure for dandruff.

Adding sheen
Beer used as a final rinse acts as a setting lotion and will help make your child's hair shiny.

Rinsing out tangles
If you rinse your child's hair with wine vinegar, that will remove any last traces of soap and make it silkier and easy to comb.

Queen, Queen Caroline,
Washed her hair in turpentine,
Turpentine to make it shine,
Queen, Queen Caroline.
NURSERY RHYME

THE FIRST CLIP

There is an almost universal belief that premature nail-cutting is unlucky, and if a child's nails get too long they should be bitten off. Indeed, many say that a child should never have his nails cut before he is one year old or he will become "light-fingered". Most mothers find that a child's toenails rarely need cutting before then, as they just break off.

STEALTHY CUTTING

Once your child is older, if you are nervous about trimming his fingernails, cut them when he is asleep – using the special scissors you can buy for cutting children's nails, which are sharp enough to do the job but have rounded ends.

NAIL NOTCHING

Cut fingernails to a round shape. Toenails should be cut straight across, with just the corners rounded, to avoid ingrowing toenails. If they should become ingrown, cut a notch in the middle of the nail. The nail will close the notch, thus drawing the nail away from the sides and toward the middle.

Cut them on Monday, you cut them for health;
Cut them on Tuesday, you cut them for wealth;
Cut them on Wednesday, you cut them for news;
Cut them on Thursday, a new pair of shoes;
Cut them on Friday, you cut them for sorrow;
Cut them on Saturday, see your true-love tomorrow;
Cut them on Sunday, you cut them for evil,
For all the next week you'll be ruled by the devil.
NURSERY RHYME

NOSE-RUBBING

If your child has something such as a pea or a small marble stuck up his nose, never put anything else (including your finger) up his nose in an attempt to retrieve it. Instead, gently rub the outside of his nose by the bridge and slowly work the object out.

Nose-rubbing was also put to good use in the last century. Mothers were advised that if a baby had a stuffed-up nose, rubbing a little tallow on the bridge last thing at night would help him breathe more freely.

TALLOW Melted animal fat used for making candles and soap and for greasing machinery.

DEALING WITH A NOSEBLEED

Slipping a large door key down the back of a child who has a nosebleed is supposed to stop the bleeding. However, the nosebleed will normally stop of its own accord after ten minutes or so. While the blood continues to flow, either place a basin below the child's nose to catch the drips or get him to wipe his nose gently from time to time with a cold damp cloth. If you apply a cold damp cloth to the bridge of his nose, that may help too.

CLOSE FOCUS

In the 1950s mothers were advised not to hang things from the hood of the baby carriage, since it was not good for a baby to focus all the time on objects close to his eyes. This still makes sense. If you give him the opportunity to look at the clouds and trees, and at your face as you press it close up to his, his eyes will get all the exercise they need.

STICKY EYES

For the first year of a child's life, always wash his eyes with previously boiled and cooled water. Use a fresh piece of absorbent cotton for each eye and wash from the outer corner towards the nose.

In the 1940s mothers were told to bathe the crust off sticky eyelids with absorbent cotton and a warm salt solution (1 teaspoon of salt to 1 pint of water), again working from the outer corner of each eye inwards.

At one time, if a baby was born with sticky eyes that was supposed to be a sign of inherited syphilis – which, of course, it was not.

BITING ON CORAL

Because weaning was only started once the first tooth had arrived and because once weaning had begun so many children died from malnutrition, people confused the dangers of an inadequate diet and lack of hygiene with the relatively minor problems of teething (known as the "breeding of teeth").

The breeding of teeth was considered to be a necessary evil, for which a mother needed help in order to make sure that her child survived. Red coral, in particular, was believed to offer magic protection and a coral stick was often given to the baby to act as a teething ring. So special was the coral that if the child became critically ill it was supposed to turn pale and only revive its colour when the child recovered. Even today a coral necklace is still popular as a girl's christening present, and Queen Elizabeth II of England appears in many childhood photographs wearing hers.

Nowadays it is understood that teething is a part of normal childhood development and that, as it goes on for roughly two years, it is bound to coincide with many common childhood diseases although it cannot be held responsible for any of them.

TEETHING TROUBLES

Superstition was rife in the world of tooth breeding. It was believed that if the first tooth arrived in the lower jaw (which it had a fifty-fifty chance of doing), the child would die in childhood. In parts of England a gap between the two front teeth large enough to put a coin through indicated that a child would be rich – but in north-east Scotland it was a sign that, when grown-up, the child would like the opposite sex too much for his or her own good. Even today some mothers burn each of their child's milk teeth as they fall out. This custom is derived from an ancient tradition. Originally it was feared that if the tooth was simply thrown away a witch might find it, whereas burning the tooth would dispose of it for good.

> *"Adam and Eve had many advantages, but the principal one was that they escaped teething."*
>
> MARK TWAIN (1835-1910)

Agate Iron Bed Pans.

45192   Agate Iron   Bed Pans,   like cut. Each..$2.04

DIRE MEASURES

The Siriono of South America never punish a child that urinates or defecates on his parents while he is being carried around. Toilet training is only started once the child can walk, and it is done with much encouragement and no punishment.

In the West, "the bowel movement" has taken on an exaggerated importance. Not so long ago, if results were not forthcoming a potty-obsessed nanny would insert her finger up into the bowels of her charge and say that she could "feel it there", so why didn't the child let it out? One late-Victorian doctor, Dr. William Arbuthnot Lane, is known to have simply removed the entire colon, thus making constipation impossible.

HABIT TRAINING

There is not much historical information about toilet training and how it was achieved. Indeed, Victorian instructions that have survived are so coy as to be almost non-existent. Reading between the lines, it would appear that toilet training has remained much the same over the centuries, with parents often as worried about it then as they can be now. It was begun at three months, or earlier, with long periods on the pot and sustained efforts by the parent or nurse to try and make the child appreciate the virtues of cleanliness. If the pot was empty, then laxatives such as syrup of figs or castor oil, or even enemas, would be used to achieve the desired result.

A 1920s mothercraft manual discusses and dismisses toilet training in five paragraphs. It was probably the first book to mention the subject openly, although it appears in the index disguised as "habit training". Pavlov's work on "conditioning" had clearly made a great impression. The manual suggested that the new baby be put on the pot once he was three days old. And four days after that there would be no more soiled nappies – ever! Presumably the cold rim of the pot was expected to trigger off a motion. This, of course, was impossible, but in some ways the manual was very modern. It insisted that "care must be taken not to lay too much stress on this habit-training, or to scold infants if they dirty or wet themselves; in many cases such over-emphasis has produced a psychological difficulty."

Today pot-training methods vary. Some argue that it is best to wait until the child himself suggests a desire to go to the pot. Others maintain that regular potting after meals once the child has reached nine months is best (rather than the three days suggested above), and it certainly means fewer dirty nappies to change.

Chambers.
45191 Chambers, Agate Iron Ware.
Size 7x4⅛ 8½x4⅞ 9¾x5½
Each 53c. 68c. 85c.

A SPOONFUL OF HONEY

Honey is an excellent cure for many things. A spoonful of honey will help soothe a sore throat or cough and cure a cold. Honey rubbed on the skin reduces bruising and helps cuts and scrapes to heal. In the 1930s, they believed that mixing half a teaspoon of powdered borax with a tablespoon of honey would cure both cracked lips and a sore throat.

AND ONE OF COD-LIVER OIL

Children used to be plied with cod-liver oil almost religiously, as it contained both Vitamin A and Vitamin D. The baby was given about five drops a day at first, increasing to a teaspoon per day by the time he was eight weeks old.

In a childcare book published during the 1940s, the young mother was advised that most children *really* liked their cod-liver oil. Moreover, she should avoid "pulling a face" when administering it to baby and try not to to "prejudice him against it" in any way.

DEALING WITH HICCUPS

Often mothers can feel their babies hiccupping in the womb. Babies also have fits of hiccups when very, very young that go away without any intervention. Hiccupping doesn't usually worry a child until he is a few years old – then it's worth trying some of the traditional remedies. To make a child's hiccups disappear, get him to try one or more of the following:

- Eat a large spoon of granulated sugar.
- Eat a small piece of ice.
- Drink directly from the tap rather than from a glass.
- Hold his breath and swallow quickly several times.
- Drink a glass of water from the wrong side of the glass (the side furthest away from the drinker).
- Gargle with plain water for a minute or two.

WASP AND BEE STINGS

Rub onion on wasp stings to take away the pain and put lemon or lime juice or baking-soda-and-water paste on bee stings. Placing a copper coin on a wasp or bee sting, preferably without delay, sometimes eases the pain – and is certainly worth trying when other remedies aren't immediately available.

TEMPERATURE TAKING

The best way to take a baby's temperature is in the groin. Just place the thermometer in the fold of the groin, cross one of the child's legs over the other, keeping a gentle but firm hold on both of them, and leave the thermometer in place for a minute.

Alternatively, buy a thermometer that you can simply stick on his forehead. Never take a child's temperature in the rectum – the thermometer can break.

BRINGING DOWN A FEVER

If a child has a high temperature, in hot countries bags of ice are wrapped in a towel and placed on his head.

Another way to bring a sick child's temperature down is to dip a wash cloth into a mixture of white vinegar and water, then wring it out and place it on his forehead.

WALKING THROUGH TREES

In the eighteenth century trees that split down the middle were believed to have healing powers. If a sick child walked through the gap naked and the two halves of the tree were then tightly bound together again, the child would regain strength as the tree's wound healed. The cure was reputed to be effective for healing rickets and other debilitating conditions. The only drawback was that the tree could not be felled – otherwise the child's disease would return.

Ring a ring o'roses,
A pocket full of posies,
A-tishoo! A-tishoo!
We all fall down.

NURSERY RHYME

A GRISLY RHYME

Luckily we live in a time when serious childhood illnesses are no longer commonplace and it is possible to immunize children against many infantile diseases. In the past, as well as terrible endemic illnesses such as smallpox, diphtheria, whooping cough, tuberculosis and rickets, there were also unexpected plagues and epidemics that came from abroad. One of the most deadly of these swept through Asia and the whole of Europe before arriving in England in 1348. It was later known as the Black Death. Coughing and sneezing were accompanying symptoms, and scholars have suggested that the nursery rhyme printed above was a folk memory of the disease.

RING The spots covering the bodies of the stricken were ring-shaped.

POSIES It was believed that carrying a nosegay would ward off the plague.

FAMILY THERAPY

In Suffolk, England, if several children from the same family were stricken with whooping cough a curious remedy was tried. A lock of hair from the eldest girl's head was cut off and put in milk, which the other children then drank, starting from the youngest and working upwards. It was believed that the whooping cough would then leave the household.

TAKE A POWDER

When a child in Sri Lanka has mumps, an ancient cure is for his parents to scrape a dead elephant's jaw bone, then mix the bone powder with lemon juice and apply the mixture to the swelling. It is said to smell horrible but relieve the pain.

GRANDMOTHER'S REMEDIES

Coughing
A tablespoon of glycerine in a mug of hot milk will often stop a fit of coughing.

Headaches
The juice of a lemon, without sugar, drunk before breakfast can make a headache vanish.

Burns
Cold tea leaves bound on a minor burn will reduce the burning sensation.

Diarrhoea
A traditional cure for diarrhoea is to give a stricken child a teaspoonful of strawberry-leaf tea (1 ounce of washed fresh leaves to 1 pint of boiling water) every two or three hours "while necessity continues."

Bruises
If your child shuts his finger in a door or bruises himself badly, put his finger in as hot water as he can manage, without scalding him, for at least fifteen minutes. Keep on topping up the water so it stays hot.

6

ALL PLAY AND NO WORK

No matter how many toys you give your child, if it isn't the right toy for his particular stage of development it will mean  nothing to him. Very often the "toys" you find at home (the wooden spoons, the empty coffee cans without sharp edges, or old rolls of wallpaper and crayons) are the best toys a child can have. He may get as much fun out of a play house or truck improvised from a cardboard box as from expensive plastic ones bought at a toy store.

All work and no play makes Jack a dull boy;
All play and no work makes Jack a mere toy.
TRADITIONAL SAYING

ROCK-A-BYE BABY

In the days of swaddling, it was soon realized that babies weren't getting any exercise – so special nurses called "rockers" were employed to bounce the infant around on their laps in the hope that this would provide enough exercise to prevent him from getting rickets. In 1612 a French doctor advised that once the baby was three weeks old this "exercise" should be taken out of doors so the child was exposed to some sun. This led to rockers treating the swaddled baby rather like a basket ball and, instead of just jiggling him around on their knees, they would throw him to each other to relieve their boredom. It also led to tragedy – in the early sixteenth century the younger brother of the future French king Henry IV was flung to death, being "rocked" out of a top-floor window.

By the nineteenth century it was understood that if a baby is placed alternately on his back and front on a flat surface he will exercise himself by stretching, sprawling and kicking; and that taking him outside would give him fresh surroundings to look at, to stimulate his brain. One book in the 1940s suggested that fathers should play a part in exercising the baby by moving his legs round and round, as if cycling, and gently jiggling him up and down on their knees "until he gurgles with laughter." The manual recommended two exercise periods a day: one before and during the morning bath, and one before tea time.

LIBERATING THE MOTHER

The idea of confining a baby in a contraption in which he can amuse himself, while his mother gets on with her own life, is not new – and has not always been approved of. In the fifteenth century children some-times spent hours in their chairs, which resembled the high chairs of today. Some were equipped with a potty in the seat, others had a small charcoal heater fitted in the base so the infant would not get cold. They all had a bar across the arms, so the more adventurous child could not escape, and sometimes a little tray was attached to accommodate food and toys.

PLAYPENS AND CRASH HELMETS

Regimen for Young Children, published in the fifteenth century, suggested that parents should construct a little pen of leather to put the child in once he began to crawl. A century later, the first drawings of "the Pudding" appeared. This was a crash helmet that encircled the baby's head to protect it from knocks and bruises. Made of padded cloth, it was held on by strings that tied under the child's chin. Puddings went out of fashion in the early 1800s – but are now once again being worn by children in France.

BABY WALKERS

Baby walkers allowed the baby some degree of liberty, as he sat in a frame mounted on wheels that held him upright while he "walked" around. They were popular in Britain and Europe in the fifteenth century, and still are today although now made from metal and plastic rather than willow.

Baby walkers can tire legs that are not yet ready for walking. They have also been known to tip over, and there are stories of children that have fallen down stairs or into blazing fires while roaming the world in a baby walker. If used at all, baby walkers have to be used with care.

THEIR OWN SPACE

Today it is accepted that if a child cannot have his own nursery or playroom he should at least be given an area somewhere in the house that is his and his alone. However, the idea that children need their own space to develop and ought to be free to play without being constantly reprimanded is by no means new:

"The nursery is a child's own domain; it is his castle, and he should be Lord Paramount therein. If he choose to blow a whistle, or to spring a rattle, or to make any other hideous noise, which to him is sweet music, he should be allowed, without let or hindrance to do so. If any members of the family have weak nerves let them keep at a respectful distance."

From ADVICE TO A MOTHER by PYE HENRY CHAVASSE, c.1914

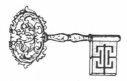

TREASURED POSSESSIONS

The story goes that the Brontë children had no toys except a key. Nevertheless, this doesn't seem to have stunted their development.

Often the toys that are most fun are found ones – sticks found in the park that can be pulled along behind as railway carriages, placed between the knees as hobby horses, or cuddled and put to bed as dolls. But for those children who cannot be outdoors all day, collecting leaves, building tree houses, and throwing stones into puddles, toys are a necessity.

Modern parents tend to shower their children with toys at every opportunity. But no child needs hundreds of toys: and if they are all out on display at the same time, they lose something of their special, individual appeal. If toys are given to a young child in rotation, so that each day some are put away and others are brought out, then they tend to be more highly treasured and their appeal lasts much longer.

In the Victorian poem below, a father describes the toys his son has put close to his bed before going to sleep. They show both the imagination of the child and his lack of bought toys.

He had put, within his reach,
A box of counters and a red-veined stone,
A piece of glass abraded by the beach,
And six or seven shells,
A bottle with bluebells
And two French copper coins, ranged there with
careful art,
To comfort his sad heart.

From "THE TOYS" by COVENTRY PATMORE (1823-96)

HIS AND HERS

Why shouldn't a boy derive satisfaction from threading beads and making necklaces? Or a girl enjoy playing with a train set?

The idea that girls and boys should have their own toys and colours is a relatively new one. When, in the seventeenth century, the future King Charles I of England figured in a painting of the royal family holding a doll, no one would have thought it the slightest bit odd.

The idea that girls learn housekeeping from playing with dolls and dolls' houses is not new either and was certainly flourishing by the nineteenth century.

When I was sick and lay a-bed,
I had two pillows at my head,
And all my toys beside me lay
To keep me happy all the day.

And sometimes for an hour or so
I watched my leaden soldiers go,
With different uniforms and drills,
Among the bed-clothes, through the hills;

And sometimes sent my ships in fleets
All up and down among the sheets;
Or brought my trees and houses out,
And planted cities all about.

I was the giant great and still
That sits upon the pillow-hill,
And sees before him, dale and plain,
The pleasant land of counterpane.

"THE LAND OF COUNTERPANE"
by ROBERT LOUIS STEVENSON (1850-94)

THE VALUE OF TOYS

In the nineteenth century parents began to realize that play had an educational value. Before then, play was regarded as something that young children would do and should then grow out of. One typical Victorian lady expressed the view that "perfect play is the anticipation of perfect work," and she and the rest of her contemporaries believed that play could teach children how to be industrious.

But even before that, some toys had been designed as educational tools. ABC blocks were invented during the reign of Elizabeth I; and Charles I was given a small rocking horse so that he could learn the basics of riding before being put on a live horse. Jigsaws were invented in 1760, by a geography teacher as a handy teaching aid.

THE GREAT OUTDOORS

"Let the amusements of a child be as much as possible out of doors... Do not let him be always poring over books."

From ADVICE TO A MOTHER by PYE HENRY CHAVASSE, c.1914

Books! 'tis a dull and endless strife,
Come, hear the woodland linnet!
How sweet his music! On my life
There's more of wisdom in it.

And hark! how blithe the throstle sings!
He, too, is no mean preacher:
Come forth into the light of things –
Let Nature be your teacher.

WILLIAM WORDSWORTH (1770-1850)

BOYS AND GIRLS COME OUT TO PLAY

Children have always played in the street outside their house, and parents have always worried (and complained) about it. In the seventeenth century, a beadle was hired to beat away the "unlucky boys with toys and balls" that were playing near the Royal Exchange in London. Earlier still, in 1332, children cavorting in the grounds of the Palace of Westminster were so rowdy that it was considered necessary to ban them from playing there while Parliament was sitting.

BEADLE An official who kept order – in effect an early police constable.

Sour Sweets.

Boys and girls come out to play,
The moon doth shine as bright as day.
Leave your supper and leave your sleep,
And join your playfellows in the street.
Come with a whoop and come with a call,
Come with a good will or not at all.
Up the ladder and down the wall,
A half-penny loaf will serve us all;
You find milk, and I'll find flour,
And we'll have a pudding in half an hour.
NURSERY RHYME

Leap Frog

THE RULES OF THE GAME

While play has unlimited boundaries, games have rules. Many games are over 2,000 years old and, thanks to children's love of detail, have been passed down from child to child in almost the original form. Children in Ancient Greece played hide-and-seek (*Apodidraskinda*), tug of war (*Dielkustinda*), and blindman's buff (*Muinda*).

Piggyback fighting is vividly depicted in illuminated medieval manuscripts, and medieval children are known to have played marbles. Bowls, hide-and-seek (which was called "King by your Leave"), and tug of war ("Sunne and Moone") were enjoyed in Elizabethan times. A book published in 1688 mentioned "Battledore and Shuttle cock", "Hide and seech", and "Hop skotches"; and in 1744 *A Little Pretty Pocket-Book*, one of the earliest books on how to keep children amused, included references to cricket and "Base-Ball".

Many of the rules in children's games have their roots in the past, too. The custom of spinning the "blindman" round three times in blindman's buff was already well-established in the seventeenth century. Older still is the idea that making an agreed sign or uttering a certain word, such as "pax", entitles you to a breathing space during a game. This seems to have originated in the Middle Ages: during prolonged warfare the Church would impose a period of respite, known as "the truce of God", when all fighting had to cease.

MADE FOR PLAY

Play is a vital part of childhood and of growing up – a means of testing, exploring, imagining, and being.

"What an unnatural thing it is to confine a child several hours a day to his lessons; why, you might as well put a colt in harness and make him work for his living! A child is made for play; his roguish little eye, his lithe figure, his antics, and his drollery, all indicate that he is cut out for play – that it is as necessary to his existence as the food he eats and as the air he breathes!"

From ADVICE TO A MOTHER by PYE HENRY CHAVASSE, c.1914

"Children should be…wisely guided by the one in charge, who should enter into all the childish 'make believes' and not condemn them as 'stupid'. The child with an imagination lives a wonderful life and should be helped to follow all natural instincts wisely."

From THE MOTHERCRAFT MANUAL by MABEL LIDDIARD, 1923

7

SPARE THE ROD

CHILDHOOD is for growing, developing, and learning in a safe environment, surrounded by love and approval. A child needs to feel secure as he explores the world, for every day he finds himself confronted with unfamiliar objects, concepts and situations. A confident child will be a confident adult, able to cope with the tensions and complexities of the modern world.

When mother calls, obey,
Do not loiter, do not stay.
Hasten child, be quick,
Do not want another kick.

NURSERY RHYME

Afterwards, when both were wives
With children of their own;
Their mother-hearts beset with fears,
Their lives bound up in tender lives...
From GOBLIN MARKET by CHRISTINA ROSSETTI (1830-94)

THE WORRIES OF PARENTHOOD

Being a parent is not easy, although somehow we all cope. All parents have ambiguous feelings towards their children, adoring them one minute and being short-tempered with them the next – then spending much time feeling guilty about not being able to simply love them 24 hours a day.

Parents have long worried about whether they are going to "make a good job" of bringing up their children. Most parents not only care about their child today but also in the future. Some have goals for their child and worry constantly about how to ensure that those goals are attained. In 1835, six months after the birth of her daughter Marianne, the novelist Elizabeth Gaskell began to write a diary. In it she expresses her concern about Marianne's future, and also about her own inadequacies as a mother:

"In general she is so good...the materials put into my hands are so excellent, and beautiful...it seems to increase my responsibility. If I should misguide her from carelessness or neglect...from ignorance and errors in judgement...I know I may, and probably shall, very often."
From THE DIARY of ELIZABETH GASKELL (1810-65)

GOOD-ENOUGH PARENTING

Throughout history mothers have rarely, if they could afford it, been full-time mothers. The wet nurse was the first mother's help, often taking the child away from the family at birth and returning him only when he was three years old. Since then there have been nurses and, in more recent times, nannies, au pairs, and child minders.

The difference is that Freud, Jung, Klein and others have made parents uncomfortably aware of the supposed "damage" that can be done to a child in the first three years, and especially the first six months, of life if he does not receive enough of the right kind of mother-love. Consciousness of such considerations has placed an immense burden of guilt on the shoulders of all but the most insensitive mother. Terms such as "bonding" and "quality time" and "the perfect mother" are symptomatic of the pressures brought to bear on the twentieth-century mother. Perhaps the best label is "the good-enough mother", which is what all mothers are; and if you leave your children in the hands of someone prepared to give them the unquestioning love they need, then you should be able to go out to work with a clear conscience.

"Children begin by loving their parents.
After a time they judge them.
Rarely, if ever, do they forgive them."
From A WOMAN OF NO IMPORTANCE by OSCAR WILDE, 1893

GREAT EXPECTATIONS

Parents have always held high hopes for their children, and often been disappointed. Nowadays, it is taken for granted that daughters may achieve as much as their brothers, and their education has improved. However, in the mid seventeenth century the notion of a girl learning practically anything was considered by many a "vice". Women were not expected to have much knowledge, and were supposed to live "in obedience" rather than independently. In 1651 an English girl keen to learn Latin, Greek, and Hebrew was told by her godfather not to be "so covetous" of the knowledge of men. Knowledge of her mother tongue, possibly plus French, was thought more becoming.

In the early nineteenth century even religious education was problematic, since some parents felt that the Bible was not entirely suitable for girls. Generally, daughters were schooled in music, singing, needlework, writing, dancing, and French; and sons were given a solid classical education, with much time spent on Latin, Greek, ancient history, and geography (plus science from the mid nineteenth century onwards).

*Every baby born into the world
is a finer one than the last.*
From NICHOLAS NICKLEBY by CHARLES DICKENS (1812-70)

*"I wrote several letters to announce my son's birth.
I indulged some imaginations that he might
perhaps be a great man."*
From THE DIARY of JAMES BOSWELL (1740-95)

Here's Sulky Sue,
What shall we do?
Turn her face to the wall
Till she comes to.
NURSERY RHYME

TOO MANY TANTRUMS

All children have tantrums, and most mothers work out their own ways of coping with them. The best way of avoiding them is to be consistent in your behaviour and, if humanly possible, remain calm. If your child knows what his boundaries are, and you treat him predictably, gently, and with respect at all times, tears and temper may be comparatively rare.

Confronted with a tantrum, different parents resort to different strategies. Some put the child straight into his bedroom, where he is left alone until he has stopped crying. Some hug the offended child reassuringly until he has calmed down. Some try to distract him with a long-forgotten or much-loved toy, and others try whispering in his ear in the hope that he'll quiet down to hear what they are saying.

Always try to avoid confrontations. If it is a trivial dispute, it won't hurt to let him have his own way. Otherwise, at least grant him the same courtesy and consideration you would display towards an adult.

SPOILING THE CHILD

Throughout the ages parents have been frightened of "spoiling" their children, by which they mean that they are worried about having been indulgent – and most parents are guilty of that.

"We learn from daily experience, that children who have been the least indulged, thrive much better, unfold all their faculties quicker, and acquire more muscular strength and vigour of mind, than those who have been constantly favoured, and treated by their parents with the most solicitous attention."

From ENQUIRE WITHIN UPON EVERYTHING, 1877

NOTHING WILL COME OF NOTHING

"Naughty" comes from naughty, naught, nothing. The implication being that a child who was naughty was bad, evil, worthless, nothing.

A JOLLY RIDE.

WHIZ KIDS

"That energy which makes a child hard to manage is the energy which afterward makes him a manager of life."

HENRY WARD BEECHER, CONGREGATIONAL MINISTER (1813-87)

GENTLE TEACHING

St. Anselm, the eleventh-century bishop, was once approached by an abbot for advice about the way the boys in his cloister were behaving. "What pray, can we do with them? They are perverse and incorrigible; day and night we cease not to chastise them, yet they grow daily worse and worse." When Anselm asked what kind of men they became, the abbot admitted that the boys grew into "dull and brutish" adults. To which, Anselm gently replied:

"Is there no way but that of stripes and scourges for shaping them to be good? Did you ever see a goldsmith shape his gold or silver plate into a fair image by blows alone? I doubt it. To give the plate its proper shape he will first press it gently and tap it with his tools; then again he will more softly raise it with discreet pressure from below, and caress it into shape. So should you behave with your boys."

LORDS OF THE WORLD

Jean-Jacques Rousseau, the eighteenth-century French philosopher, was much in favour of the child. His view was that the newborn baby was essentially good, although of course very susceptible to evil corruption. Punishment, he argued, should be avoided. Instead, children ought to be treated as princes and allowed to do what they will.

The result was an outbreak of mischief. According to Rousseau's enemies, one child, having first obtained his father's permission, was carried into the dining room astride the family luncheon (a saddle of mutton) with his feet dangling in the gravy.

SECURITY, LOVE AND A FIRM HAND

Thankfully, by the 1940s repression was unfashionable and the Victorians' "teaching of obedience" was no longer considered proper. However, one manual was brave enough to stick its neck out and disagree with popular opinion. It condemned as "false psychological jargon" the fashionable idea that giving a child complete freedom would allow him to develop to the full. Controversially for the time, it suggested that a child needed security, love, guidance, and a firm parental background in order to survive.

Happily there are now anti-smacking groups that are campaigning against any physical abuse of children, not just against baby-battering. There should never be any need to hit a child, no matter what he has done. But if, faced with some infantile outrage, you do resort to smacking, don't let yourself be tormented by the feeling that you've committed an unspeakable crime.

SPARING THE ROD

He that spareth his rod hateth his son;
but he that loveth him chasteneth him betimes.
PROVERBS XIII, 24

"I have given you, forsooth, kisses in plenty,
and but few stripes. If ever I have flogged you
'twas but with a peacock's tail."
SIR THOMAS MORE, LAWYER, STATESMAN AND SAINT (1478-1535)

CRIME AND PUNISHMENT

Children must be able to learn by example and by praise, although inevitably a parent may sometimes wish to give out a harmless yet memorable punishment to an older child. In the 1870s a young woman, Mary Hughes, wrote about the most dreaded punishment her brothers received – having their hair cut. It was not the haircut which was so bad, but the three-quarters of an hour wait in which there was "nothing to do but stare at a fern and a picture of Cromwell sitting at his daughter's death-bed." Mrs Hughes certainly knew how to punish her sons.

A less-Victorian turn-of-the-century expert stated that he would only flog a child for two offenses: playing with fire or telling lies.

A SHORT SHARP SHOCK

Aztec boys that misbehaved would be beaten, pricked with the spiny leaves of a large maguey cactus, and bound hand and foot. They were then either laid naked on the wet ground for 24 hours or held over a fire of chilli peppers and made to inhale the acrid smoke. Girls were either punished in a similar manner or made to do extra household chores.

WHO'S BOSS?

In Ohio in the early nineteenth century a law was passed stipulating that a father would have to pay a $10 fine each time he hit his child. It is known that one twelve-year-old boy, thrashed for lying, took his father to court – and others may have followed suit.

KISS HIM BETTER

After punishing a child, however justly, parents often later regret it – as did the writer of this tender poem:

My little Son, who looked from thoughtful eyes
And moved and spoke in quiet grown-up wise,
Having my law the seventh time disobeyed,
I struck him, and dismissed
With hard words and unkissed,
His Mother, who was patient, being dead.
Then, fearing lest his grief should hinder sleep,
I visited his bed,
But found him slumbering deep,
With darkened eyelids, and their lashes yet
From his late sobbing wet.
And I, with moan,
Kissing away his tears, left others of my own.

From "THE TOYS" by COVENTRY PATMORE (1823-96)

A babe is fed with milk and praise.

From THE FIRST TOOTH by
CHARLES LAMB (1775-1834) and MARY LAMB (1764-1847)

A WORD IN PRIVATE

In 1849 a sensitive upper-middle-class lady wrote that it was important to correct one's children "as little as possible" before others. If an admonishment was necessary, then one should "speak to them privately." She had quite rightly observed that a "loud reproof may sometimes provoke wrath instead of leading to repentance." However, she did admit that on occasion "instant rebuke is needful."

Unless you are 100 per cent sure your child will obey you, never shout at him in public. It can be very humiliating if he takes no notice. In fact, it is best not to shout at your child at all – he'll only be tempted to imitate your aggressiveness, and yelling at someone is a very repressive means of getting one's own way.

A little praise works better than a lot of nagging.
TRADITIONAL SAYING

GROWING UP

Growing up can be a tricky business. In the initiation ceremony of one primitive tribe, a son had to copulate with his mother in order to be considered an adult. In another, from the age of fourteen it was customary for a boy to take a mistress much older than himself and live with her until he reached the age of marriage.

For most of us the boundary between childhood and adulthood is more straightforward, and the rites of passage somewhat less daunting. Until recently, in many parts of the world twenty-one was the legal age of responsibility. Today, in most countries, adulthood officially begins at eighteen.

DEDICATED TO MY NANNY, JEAN SMITH

The author wishes to thank:
Leslie Elliott for her help, advice and encouragement.

The author and editors gratefully acknowledge the following:
Advice to a Mother, Pye Henry Chavasse, Cassell *c.*1914
Art for Commerce, Scolar Press 1973
Art in Advertising, The Press Art School 1921
Brewer's Dictionary of Phrase and Fable, Ivor H. Evans, Cassell 1986
Cassell's Family Magazine, Cassell 1894
A Celebration of Babies, ed. Sally Emerson, Blackie 1986
The Child, the Family and the Outside World, D.W. Winnicott, Tavistock 1957
Children's Games, Iona & Peter Opie, OUP 1984
Dearest Child (Queen Victoria's letters to Princess Vicky), ed. R. Fulford, Evans 1964
Dearest Hope: An Anthology on Children and Parents, Oxfam Publications 1977
The Domestic Life of Thomas Jefferson, ed. Sarah Randolph, Harper & Bros. 1871
The Dover Pictorial Archive Series
Down the Santa Fe Trail and Into Mexico, Susan Magoffin, Yale 1926
The Encyclopaedia of Illustrations, Studio Editions 1990
The Encyclopedia of Superstitions, E. & M.A. Radford & C. Hole, Hutchinson 1975
Enquire Within Upon Everything, Houlston & Sons 1877
The Everyday Book and Table Book, William Hone, Thomas Tegg 1826
Everyday Life of the Aztecs, Warwick Bray, Batsford 1968
Everyman's Book of English Verse, ed. John Wain, Dent 1981
From Kitchen to Garret, Jane Ellen Panton, Ward & Downey 1888
Good Housekeeping's Baby Book, National Magazine Company 1944
The History of Childhood, Lloyd de Mause, Souvenir Press 1976
A History of Infant Feeding, Ian G. Wickes, BMA 1953
The Iconographic Encyclopaedia of Science, Literature and Art, 1851
(reprinted as *The Complete Encyclopedia of Illustration* by Merehurst Press 1988)
Indian Boyhood, Charles A. Eastman, 1902 (reprinted by Dover Publications 1971)
The International Thesaurus of Quotations, ed. Rhoda Thomas Tripp, Crowell 1970
(reprinted by Penguin Books 1976)
A Lasting Relationship, Linda Pollock, Fourth Estate 1987
The Letters of Mark Twain, ed. Albert Bigelow Paine, Chatto & Windus 1920
Letters on Different Subjects, Lady Sarah Pennington, J.Walter 1770
The Life and Letters of Elizabeth Prentiss, G.L. Prentiss, Hodder & Stoughton 1882
Life in the Middle Ages, G.G. Coulton, CUP 1967
The Lore and Language of Schoolchildren, Iona & Peter Opie, OUP 1972
Mary Ellen's Best of Helpful Hints, Warner Books 1979
The Masterpiece: The Works of Aristotle the Famous Philosopher
(reprinted by Moritz & Chambers – undated)
Montgomery Ward & Co. 1895 Catalogue (reprinted by Dover Publications 1969)
The Mother's Companion, S.W. Partridge & Co. 1888
The Mothercraft Manual, Mabel Liddiard, Churchill 1923
Nanny Says, Hugh Casson & Joyce Grenfell, Souvenir Press 1987
The "Olio" Cookery Book (revised edition), L. Sykes, Ernest Benn 1928
The Oxford Dictionary of Quotations (third edition), OUP 1979
The Oxford Dictionary of Superstitions, ed. Iona Opie & Moira Tatem, OUP 1989
The Oxford Nursery Rhyme Book, Iona & Peter Opie OUP 1987
Pocket Guide to Practical Babycare, Christine Bruell, Mitchell Beazley 1985
Pregnancy, Gordon Bourne, Cassell 1972 (reprinted by Pan Books 1975)
Pregnancy Week by Week, Nina Grunfeld, Conran/Octopus 1991
The Puffin Book of Nursery Rhymes, Iona & Peter Opie, Puffin Books 1980
The Rise and Fall of the British Nanny, Jonathan Gathorne-Hardy, Weidenfeld 1985
Sears Roebuck 1908 Catalogue (reprinted by DBI Books 1971)
Spot Check, Nina Grunfeld & Mike Wilks, World's Work 1984
Stevenson's Book of Quotations, Cassell/Dodd Mead 1934
The Sunday Friend, Mowbray & Co. 1893
Tried Favourites Cookery Book, Mrs E.W. Kirk, Horace Marshall & Son 1940
What a Young Man Ought to Know, Sylvanus Stall, The Vir Publishing Co. 1904
Woman at Home, George Newnes 1912
The Woman's Book, T.C. & E.C. Jack 1911
Yesterday's Babies, Diana Dick, Bodley Head 1987